HOW TO BLESS A MISSIONARY

MISSIONARY

Practical Ideas for Your Church and Family

Jennifer Brannon

How to Bless a Missionary
Copyright © 2018 Jennifer Brannon

Scripture quotations are from the ESV® Bible (The Holy Bible, English Standard Version®), copyright © 2001 by Crossway, a publishing ministry of Good News Publishers. Used by permission. All rights reserved.

Cover image taken by Jennifer Brannon. Globe pictured is produced by Replogle® Globes Partners, LLC (replogleglobes.com).
The image is used with permission.
Cover design is by German Creative.

Jennifer Brannon
Visit my website at www.familiesformissions.com

Printed in the United States of America

ISBN-13 978-0-9997991-3-0

Psalm 67
[1] *"May God be gracious to us and bless us*
and make his face to shine upon us, Selah
[2] *that your way may be known on earth,*
your saving power among all nations.
[3] *Let the peoples praise you, O God;*
let all the peoples praise you!
[4] *Let the nations be glad and sing for joy,*
for you judge the peoples with equity
and guide the nations upon earth. Selah
[5] *Let the peoples praise you, O God;*
let all the peoples praise you!
[6] *The earth has yielded its increase;*
God, our God, shall bless us.
[7] *God shall bless us;*
let all the ends of the earth fear him!"

* * *

May each family and church that reads these
pages seek to continually be a blessing to those
spreading the Good News about Jesus worldwide!

CONTENTS

INTRODUCTION

D o you wish you could be more involved in missions and play a role in spreading the Good News about Jesus? Do you wish that you could teach your kids or your church about mission work? Do you wish you could make a difference in a missionary's life?

Well, YOU CAN! Maybe you can't travel far away, and maybe you don't have much extra money. Your church budget might be small. You may feel insignificant, but you might be surprised to find out that there are many different ways that you can bless a missionary!

As a former Missionary Kid (MK), this topic is near and dear to my heart. The idea for this book was born out of an attempt to help parents of families teach their children about missions, but the idea expanded to help ministry leaders learn how to care for their missionaries. I realized that there is not much information available for those interested in this topic. This book will be a useful resource for any individual that is looking for ways to become more involved with missionaries.

Pastors and churches will find this book to be a wealth of ideas for their "Missions Sunday" or "Missions Conference".

Pastors and members of the Missions Committee can use these ideas to communicate with, and encourage, the missionaries they support.

There are a couple of terms that I would like to define for those that are new to learning about missions. When reading this book, you will see me refer to a missionary's passport country. This is the country from which the missionary was sent or where they originated. You will also notice references to the host country. This is the country where the missionary lives and serves.

I challenge you to use the pages at the end of the book to write down your favorite ideas and to track which things you have chosen and completed. This is a great way to involve the whole family, and kids will get excited about deciding together what blessing to choose next.

WHAT IS A BLESSING?

What does it mean to bless someone? Do you know what a blessing is? If we want to bless missionaries and others in our lives, we must first understand what it means to bless another person.

According to the Merriam-Webster Dictionary, *to bless* can have several meanings: to hallow or consecrate, to invoke divine care for, to be endowed with, or to confer prosperity or happiness upon. This last meaning is the one we will focus on for the purposes of this book. A *blessing*, according to the same dictionary, is an act or words that bless or a thing conducive to happiness or welfare.

So, for the purpose of blessing missionaries, we will focus on positive words and actions that will help meet their financial, psychological, and practical needs in order that they might experience financial security, a fulfilling life, and a fruitful ministry.

What are examples of blessings in the Bible? Of course, there are too many to discuss each in detail in a book such as this one, but I will briefly share some of the basics.

In the Old Testament, there are two main Hebrew words used that are typically translated as blessing. *Barak* is the first one and can mean to kneel (in adoration), to bless, to congratulate, to salute, to blaspheme, or to curse. Examples of this word can be found when God is blessing Adam (Genesis 1) and Abraham (Genesis 12 and 22), as well as scattered throughout Deuteronomy. Psalm 103 has this word many times, and this word is the one used in most of the instances when people in the Old Testament were blessing God.

> *Psalm 103:1-2, 20-22*
> [1] *"Bless the LORD, O my soul, and all that is within me, bless his holy name!*
> [2] *Bless the LORD, O my soul, and forget not all his benefits......*
> [20] *Bless the LORD, O you his angels, you mighty ones who do his word, obeying the voice of his word!*
> [21] *Bless the LORD, all his hosts, his ministers, who do his will!*
> [22] *Bless the LORD, all his works, in all places of his dominion. Bless the LORD, O my soul."*

Another word used in the Old Testament that is commonly translated as blessing is *esher*. It usually has a meaning of happiness. You can find examples of this word in Job 5:17 and Psalm 1.

Psalm 1:1-3
¹ "Blessed is the man who walks not in the counsel of
the wicked, nor stands in the way of sinners,
nor sits in the seat of scoffers;
²but his delight is in the law of the LORD, and on his
law he meditates day and night.
³He is like a tree planted by streams of water that
yields its fruit in its season, and its leaf does
not wither. In all that he does, he prospers."

In the New Testament, you can find the Greek word *makarios* which means blessed, happy, or fortunate. Examples of this word are found in the Beatitudes in Matthew 5 and Luke 6, as well as in Acts 20:35.

Acts 20:32-35
³² "And now I commend you to God and to the word of
his grace, which is able to build you up and to
give you the inheritance among all those who
are sanctified.
³³I coveted no one's silver or gold or apparel.
³⁴You yourselves know that these hands ministered to
my necessities and to those who were with me.
³⁵In all things I have shown you that by working hard
in this way we must help the weak and
remember the words of the Lord Jesus, how he
himself said 'It is more blessed to give than
receive.'"

You can also find the Greek word *eulogeo* in the New Testament. It usually means: to bless, to praise, to speak well of, or to invoke a benediction upon. Look for the word "blessing" or "bless" in Ephesians 1:3 and Romans 12:14.

> *Romans 12:14 "Bless those who persecute you; bless and do not curse them."*

So, who are we called to bless based on the examples given in Scripture? First, we should bless God. Look at Psalm 96:2, Judges 5:9, or the passage in Psalms 103. The Bible is full of examples of people who blessed and honored God. We can follow David's example in Psalm 34:1.

> *Psalm 34:1 "I will bless the Lord at all times; his praise shall continually be in my mouth."*

Several people in the Old Testament such as Moses, Isaac, Joshua, and David offered blessings to the people of God or their own families. We see an example in Joshua 22:6 where Joshua is blessing God's people.

> *Joshua 22:6 "So Joshua blessed them and sent them away, and they went to their tents."*

In passages like Romans 12:14, I Corinthians 4:12, and Luke 6:28 we also see that we are to bless those who persecute us, curse us, and revile us. This is easier said than done, but it is a goal that we can strive to achieve. We can look at Proverbs 25:22 for more wisdom on this.

*Proverbs 25:22 "If your enemy is hungry, give him
bread to eat, and if he is thirsty, give him
water to drink, for you will heap burning coals
on his head, and the Lord will reward you."*

We also see examples in the Bible of how the churches blessed Paul. One has only to look at his final parting words in Philippians to understand that the people of the Philippian church had shared in his ministry and blessed him.

Philippians 4:10-23
*[10] "I rejoiced in the Lord greatly that now at length
you have revived your concern for me. <u>You
were indeed concerned for me</u>, but you had no
opportunity.*
*[11] Not that I am speaking of being in need, for I have
learned in whatever situation I am to be
content.*
*[12] I know how to be brought low, and I know how to
abound. In any and every circumstance, I have
learned the secret of facing plenty and hunger,
abundance and need.*
[13] I can do all things through him who strengthens me.
[14] Yet it was kind of you to <u>share my trouble</u>.
*[15] And you Philippians yourselves know that in the
beginning of the gospel, when I left
Macedonia, <u>no church entered into
partnership with me in giving and receiving,
except you only</u>.*
[16] Even in Thessalonica <u>you sent me help for my needs</u>

once and again.
[17] Not that I seek the gift, but I seek the fruit that
increases to your credit.
[18] I have received full payment, and more. I am well
supplied, having received from Epaphroditus
the gifts you sent, a fragrant offering, a
sacrifice acceptable and pleasing to God.
[19] And my God will supply every need of yours
according to his riches in glory in Christ
Jesus.
[20] To our God and Father be glory forever and ever.
Amen."

All throughout Scripture we can see examples of how God blessed his followers and how they blessed each other. As part of fulfilling the Great Commission we can have many roles, but one role that is exemplified in the pages of our Bible is to bless those that are spreading the Good News about Jesus' gift of salvation. Each of us can participate in this effort and become part of the "missions team". You will learn more about this in the next chapter.

As you read the rest of the book, you will find many different ideas about how you and your church can get involved. Areas of involvement can include things like: communicating with your missionary, praying for them, taking care of the missionary's family member, helping them raise money, and providing for their needs. Each short chapter features a different concept, and you will find practical ideas that you can put into practice today!

OUR ROLE IN BLESSING MISSIONARIES

A s Believers in Jesus Christ, we are part of the Body of Christ. Our roles as part of this Body are varied - as varied as each member of the Body, but the role of the Body as a whole is spelled out in Scripture. One of the primary mandates given by Jesus to the disciples was to *"Go therefore and make disciples of all nations, baptizing them in the name of the Father and of the Son and of the Holy Spirit, teaching them to observe all that I have commanded you." Matthew 28:19-20a*

As members of the Body of Christ, we are called to both evangelism and discipleship. We should *all* be sharing Christ with those around us who have not come to trust in Jesus for their salvation, *and* we should be investing in other Christians to deepen their knowledge and understanding of God.

So, what role do we play in the worldwide mission of spreading the Good News of Jesus Christ? Jesus told his followers to go to all nations, and we see repeatedly in the Bible how God loves the nations. The problem is that all of us cannot possibly travel around the world and learn other languages to tell others about Jesus. This is where being part of the larger Body of Christ comes into play.

In 3 John, we see an example of how important John believed it was to support missionaries. He is commending Gaius for his faithful efforts to support the strangers who were going out for the sake of Jesus Christ's name. Look at the following verses in this context.

> *3 John 5-8*
> ⁵ *"Beloved, it is a faithful thing you do in all your*
> *efforts for these brothers, strangers as they are,*
> ⁶ *who testified to your love before the church. You will*
> *do well to send them on their journey in a*
> *manner worthy of God.*
> ⁷ *For they have gone out for the sake of the name,*
> *accepting nothing from the Gentiles.*
> ⁸ *Therefore we ought to support people like these, that*
> *we may be fellow workers for the truth."*

We each have different gifts and abilities provided by our Creator, and we should seek how we can use these. Spreading the Gospel around the world functions best with a team effort. The team of people that can work together to accomplish this goal includes people who:

- Train the Missionary (Skills, Language, Bible)
- Transport the Missionary
- Go to the Unreached (The Missionary)
- Send (Financial Support)
- Encourage

- Pray
- Provide services
- Manage accounts (Banking, Insurance, Bills)

Each of us can fill at least one of these roles, if not several. I encourage you to think of your specific gifts, abilities, talents, and strengths. Identify which areas fit your skills best; don't be afraid to ask for help if you are not sure. Each different role is a way that you can bless others. (The list is extensive, but could include things such as: banker, insurance agent, letter writer, childcare provider, driver, vehicle repair person, musician, photographer, graphic designer, computer technician, language expert, pilot, airplane mechanic, prayer warrior, beautician, host, cook, restauranteur, teacher, preacher, blogger, entrepreneur, donor, etc.)

In the following pages you will find practical ways that you and your church can become a blessing to a missionary. I challenge you to explore the many options in this book and find those that best match your personal abilities. Look for those that match the skillsets in your local congregation. I challenge you to think outside the box and attempt several that seem out of your comfort zone.

SECTION ONE

* * *

Communication

"Anxiety in a man's heart weighs him down,
but a good word makes him glad."
Proverbs 12:25

HOW TO BLESS A MISSIONARY

WRITE AN EMAIL TO A MISSIONARY

One of the main ways to bless a missionary is to write to them. Writing an email doesn't take much time or effort but can be a huge morale boost to a missionary serving abroad. Many missionaries are lonely for friendships. They also experience loneliness for the families and friendships that they left behind. Hearing from someone from their country of origin might be the encouragement that they need! And you don't have to be eloquent or a great writer to do this!

If you are a new person to them:
- Introduce yourself and fill them in on who you are, who your family is, what your job is, etc. They will enjoy getting to know you, even if only through an email.
- Let them know how you found out about them.
- Ask questions about their ministry or their family.
- Ask if they have specific prayer requests or needs.
- Find out when they will be in your area, and plan to meet them in person.

If you already know them:

- Just tell them what has been going on in your life.
- Remind them about your job, family, etc., in case they might not remember.
- Fill them in on important news from their home church or home city. They may have not heard that a certain person moved away or died. They might be interested to know of a local business that has expanded or shut down. Maybe send a copy of your weekly church bulletin to keep them apprised of the latest happenings.
- Tell them if local people have received awards.
- Let them know if you saw their family member doing something important or exciting. You could send a link or a copy of a newspaper or magazine article with the information. You can help them still feel connected to where they came from.
- Make sure to read the section in the next chapter on what NOT to say.

Even if you don't have a lot of time, you can still send a quick note. Just tell them you are thinking about them and praying for them. Let them know you appreciated their last newsletter or mention something that they wrote about. They will appreciate knowing that someone actually read their letter. This will encourage them a great deal, so get out there and write!

SEND A HANDWRITTEN NOTE

Texting, emailing and phone apps are great ways to communicate with someone far away. But I propose another, possibly more meaningful way. Maybe I'm a little old-fashioned, but there is something extra-special about receiving a handwritten note in the mail.

I need to provide a disclaimer that I grew up writing letters and sending them through the mail. I even had a couple of pen pals over the years. When my family went to Mexico, phone calls were very expensive (several dollars per minute), and the internet and email did not exist. Written letters were how we communicated, and we waited 6 weeks to receive them from the time they were sent. (Yes, you read that right! It took at least 6 weeks to get a letter!) This is how we received and sent information to friends, grandparents, and supporters.

Even though communication is easier and faster now, I still cherish some of those handwritten notes that I saved from past years – especially those sent by my grandma that died years ago.

Being a missionary can be, and often is, a very lonely job. A note of encouragement may be exactly what the missionary is needing to continue to learn the language, counsel someone, or continue to trudge through the forest to reach a remote people. A tangible piece of paper that they can tack up on a wall or pull out to read again and again may be one of their most valuable possessions. Did you know that some missionaries only receive one or two notes of encouragement a year? Your thoughts and prayers for them can make a huge difference!

So, get out those pens and pieces of paper. Let them know that you remember them, you are praying for them, and you know that God will encourage them. Include an encouraging passage of scripture.

What NOT to say:

- Remember to be careful about what you say in a letter to some countries that are not friendly to Christians or missionaries…you don't want to get them kicked out or thrown in jail because of something you wrote! Some countries will not allow Scripture or references to God, Jesus or the Bible. You may have to talk in a type of code language where you refer to God in third person (e.g. asking Him to help) or you may have to use misspelled words or abbreviations (e.g. prying for you).

- Do not be critical of the country or culture where the missionary lives.

- Also, some missionaries are in a country where missionaries are not allowed, and they are doing another job as their legal means of being in the country. They may be restaurant owners, business men, doctors, or resort managers. We do not want to jeopardize their position or legal status in the country with something we say.

Don't forget that you will need to check with your local post office to find out how much postage to put on your letter. One stamp will probably not be enough to send to most other countries. Ask them about how long it takes for letters to reach their destination abroad. They may not know, but you can also ask the missionary to share this with you.

Don't get discouraged if you don't hear back right away. Letters get lost more often in other countries, and it could take weeks for the letter to reach the recipient. The missionary may also be very busy with current activities, and they may not have time to write a letter and travel to the local post office to buy stamps and post it. (In some locations, this could involve several hours of travel. The missionary may only go to the post office once every few weeks.)

VISIT THEM

A great way to bless a missionary is to actually go and visit them. It can be a great encouragement to have someone from their home country come and see what they're doing and watch how they interact within the culture where they live.

Many missionaries are lonely and feel like they are trying to do the missionary work by themselves. Your visit could make them feel like they have a team behind them. They can learn that the people back home really care about what they're doing.

I think it is especially important for pastors and elders to visit missionaries. The first reason this is important is that it shows care and concern as well as an interest in their ministry. Encouraging the missionary can be accomplished with a personal visit and some verbal communication to "keep up the good work".

Secondly, these visits will allow the ministry to be observed first-hand. A visiting pastor or elder will gain invaluable insights about the work the missionary is doing as well as how the missionary lives and reacts to the environment around them. If there are concerns, they will be able to be seen and addressed appropriately.

However, there are some things to think about when you're trying to plan a visit to a missionary. The following list should help you as you make plans.

1. The first thing you should think about is **when you can go**, and you need to **find out if you have enough vacation time** from work or school to achieve this. Some people are able to use their vacation time from work and not affect their income at all. Others don't have enough vacation time and must use time without pay to do any kind of vacation or trip.

2. You also need to **check with the missionary** that you plan to visit. While a visit is very encouraging, it could also be very stressful for the missionary. You need to find out if they have free time or if it's convenient for you to visit them at the time you are planning. They may have many things already scheduled during that time. They may have a large youth conference or church conference going on, and it would not be convenient for them if you visit during those dates. Work on a date together and plan when would be the best time to visit them.

3. I strongly suggest **giving the missionary money to cover any expenses** that you will incur while you are there. Missionaries are on a fixed budget, and many of them are not financially supported well enough. So, expecting them to house you and feed you for free is not appropriate. They might be able to host a couple, a small family, or a single person with no problem at all, but you need to make plans for where people will stay and how they will be fed, especially if you're planning to take a large group. Do not expect the

missionary to foot the bill or plan everything on their own. The missionary wife should not be expected to cook for everyone the entire time you are visiting.

4. I suggest you **make a plan** to include **what you would like to do when you are visiting** the missionary. **Ask them** what they would like for you to see or do. (Don't plan a short-term trip to do something that the local people could accomplish more effectively and with less money.) Also, make sure you tell them if there are specific things you are interested in seeing. For example, if you would like to attend a church service, a youth group meeting, a small group Bible study or prayer group, they need to know this. Don't expect them to read your mind. If there are "touristy" things that you would like to do, please make sure they know about this as well. Make sure you take money to cover your expenses. Plan to pay for the missionary's expenses if they take you to see local attractions.

5. **Raise money** if you need to. Some people choose to ask friends or mail out letters asking for support. Some will have a church that supplies money for short-term mission trips. I personally do not recommend asking others for money if you are going for personal reasons and will not be working alongside the missionary to accomplish something to help them personally or in their ministry. (It seems a little bit like asking people to pay for your vacation.) Some people use money they have saved. Some people have a garage sale or sell things on online to raise funds. Some make and sell their own crafts. Get creative!

6. **Ask the missionary if they would like you to bring anything**. They might not be able to get peanut butter or chocolate chips where they live, or they might love some real graham crackers. They might need the next size clothing for their kids or a certain type of calculator or the books for next year's homeschooling curriculum. Even if they do not tell you anything, I would suggest packing something fun for them: candy, magazines, etc. I also recommend finding out what is not allowed to be brought through customs! You don't want to have the things you packed confiscated or thrown away, and you don't want to have to pay a lot of money to get them through customs.

7. **Check on medical requirements for travel**. Some countries require specific doctor's paperwork or vaccinations (and some vaccination series require several months to complete).

8. **Get your passport and apply for visas**. This can take several months to complete, so plan ahead. You can probably find a location locally that will take your passport pictures, but you will have to fill out an application and wait for the passport to arrive. This involves another cost to consider in your budgeting. It would be wise to contact the embassy where you will be traveling and let them know the dates you will be in the country, the locations where you will be, and the people you will be visiting. In case of emergencies, they can be very instrumental in helping you get home.

9. **Check weather and climate for the time of your visit.** This will help as you are preparing and packing. In many climates around the world people dress in layers, wearing something

lightweight and using a jacket or wrap over it. **Ask the missionary** you are visiting **what is appropriate to wear**. You do not want to be the only person in shorts when all other women are wearing long-sleeved shirts and skirts. You do not want to offend the local people, and you especially do not want to damage the missionary's witness among them. Dressing in a manner similar to the local people will help you not to stick out as the obvious tourist that has come to visit, and it may help you be less of a target for those with less-than-honorable intentions.

The moral of the story is: Ask the missionary! Think and pray about whether this can be an option for you, your family, or a group from your church! Consider being an encouragement to a missionary by visiting them. This may be one of the few ways that they are reassured of the team of people that are praying for them and "on their team". They will love sharing about their ministry and will love that you are able to get a first-hand view of their day-to-day life.

HOW TO BLESS A MISSIONARY

CONTACT THEM BY TELEPHONE OR VIDEO

Years ago, contacting a missionary was impossible by phone. One had to send a letter and wait months for that letter to arrive and for a response to be sent in return. I already mentioned that when my family first went to the mission field in the 1980's, it took six weeks for letters from our family and friends to reach us. Phones were available then but were very expensive – several dollars per minute.

This is not the case anymore. Communicating with people on the other side of the world is easier than ever. There are many options available for a "voice-to-voice" or "face-to-face" talk. Your missionary friend would probably be a great source of information about the best way to contact them in their current location.

You can check with your home or cell phone provider to see what your cost per minute would be to call the missionary directly. You will need to know the exact number to be dialed to reach them, including the international code and country area codes.

Another option is to contact them through Skype or another form of video chat. It can be a fun way to see the person you are talking to while you are actually talking with them. This makes it a great way to show them something or let them show you something. You will need to find out if the missionary you are wishing to contact is able to communicate this way.

There are also fun apps that you can use to contact your missionary. By using these apps, you can talk with a missionary "face-to-face" and not have costs of phone calls. Look into WhatsApp and WeChat, but there are several others, too. Investigate which one fits your needs best, and make sure you agree with how it works.

ATTEND THEIR EVENT

This may seem to be an odd chapter to include in a section on communication, but listening to a missionary speak at an event is a huge blessing to them. For the missionary, the times they share about their ministry and life in another country are some of the few times when people are willing to listen to their story and learn more.

During these meetings, the missionary can dispel the misconceptions that exist about the country where they serve. They can also help the people listening to them speak understand their ministry in more detail. Time is usually provided for people to ask questions, even if it is at the end of the session.

To better prepare for attending this session, you can read about the country or ministry of the missionary beforehand. Think of some questions that you have. Look up a craft from that country for your children to do. Your kids might even like to draw a "Welcome" picture to give to the missionary.

Ministry leaders can prepare some questions to ask the missionary. If a missionary is preaching on Sunday at your church or sharing in a Sunday School, encourage your congregation to take advantage of it! Don't let them take the Sunday "off" and decide to stay home just because it is not their normal pastor. Listen attentively and without judgment. Ask questions about things that you do not understand. You never know…you might discover your new favorite country or ministry to learn about.

ASK THEM GREAT QUESTIONS (AND LISTEN)

When communicating with a missionary, whether it be through written or verbal form, asking questions can be a big blessing or a huge source of stress. Missionaries are used to getting asked many questions, and some are fun to answer. Others are very hard to answer or downright offensive.

Asking really great questions will make the missionary realize that you are *truly interested* in learning more about them and their ministry. It will give you a window into their world and help you to understand the obstacles, problems, and blessings that they might encounter each day. It can also be a way to show them that you have insight into the issues that they might face.

Using this list could also be a great way for pastors and mission leaders of churches to draft a questionnaire to give to missionaries they support (or are considering for support). I think it is wise to have missionaries complete some questions on a yearly basis. Obviously, we do not want to overburden the missionary with busywork, but asking them some deep questions about their work and family will give us insight into their ministry and family life. It could help show areas where the missionary needs more encouragement or intervention. It could also help show areas where the ministry is growing.

Here is a list of some **great conversation starters**:
General Questions:
- Tell me how you got involved in missions.
- Tell me about how you came to believe in Jesus and trust Him as your Savior.
- What do you like best about __insert country__?
- Tell me about the culture in __insert country__.
- What are some of the things you like best about being in your "home" country?
- What are the biggest challenges you face on furlough/home assignment?
- What are your biggest challenges in the country where you serve?
- What are the obstacles you face when raising more support?
- What can I pray about for you?
- What are your greatest needs?
- What do you like to do to rest/refresh?
- How can we help you?
- What is the best way to send you a package/letter?
- What would you love to receive in a package?

- Are there things we should not include in a package or letter?
- What things are difficult or impossible for you to find in __insert country__?
- What is something that you wish you had known before going to the mission field?
- What things have supporters done that blessed you the most?

Ministry:
- Tell me about the local religions where you live.
- What are the barriers you face when sharing the gospel with others?
- What is the government position towards missionaries in __insert country__?
- What is the government's attitude toward your ministry?
- What is the response of the local people to you and your ministry?
- Tell me about some ministry successes you have had.
- Tell me about some of the biggest struggles you have had in ministry.
- How can we best pray for your ministry?

Kids and Family:
- Tell me about your kids and their lives.
- What are the biggest challenges your kids face?
- Tell me about where your kids go to school.
- What is something you enjoy doing as a family?

- What is a favorite memory that your family has experienced?
- Tell me about your friends.
- Tell me about a typical day for you/your wife/kids.
- What does your family love to eat?
- How can we best pray for your family?

Just for fun:
- If you could travel or vacation anywhere, where would you go?
- If you could do any job/vocation (other than being a missionary), what would you do?
- If you could have any talent, which would you choose?

I briefly mentioned in the beginning of this chapter that some questions are not appropriate or can seem offensive. I will draw from questions that my family was asked over the years as examples. Below you will find some questions that you **should NOT ask**:

- How much of a raise are you going to get by becoming a missionary?
- Why do you need health insurance?
- Why do you need to save for retirement?
- Are you glad to be "home"?
- Why do you need so much support…it's so cheap to live in __insert country__?
- How in the world can you live there?
- Do you eat bugs and other weird stuff?

- Do you have a dirt floor?
- (To the wife) …And what is your ministry?
- Will your wife/kids be singing/playing the piano for our services?
- What is your monthly/annual salary? (This may be appropriate for a missions committee to inquire about, but not for the average person to ask.)
- If you are having trouble raising support, don't you think that God is telling you to stop doing this ministry?
- Aren't there already way too many missionaries in _____?

As you can see, there are many questions that can be asked of a missionary, and this list obviously does not include every possible question. It is just a list to get you started thinking...and talking.

Consider how you can use the good questions. Will you see a missionary or go out to eat with them? Will you send them a letter or email? Will they visit your church? Take some time to prepare questions to ask before the next missionary visit that you will have.

HOW TO BLESS A MISSIONARY

MAKE AN INFORMATION PACKET FOR THEM

A very kind thing to have ready to give to visiting missionaries is a Welcome/Information Packet. This can be handed out to those coming to your missions conference, or you can give them out to any visiting missionary.

Items you might want to tuck into in this packet include the following:

- **A Welcome Letter**
- **Information about your church** (including contact phone numbers and email addresses for the staff and mission leaders, information on children's activities and classes, and anything else you think is important for them to know)
- **Pictures** of important people or contacts
- The **schedule of events** if there is a conference or speaking engagements

- A list of **local stores** where they can find items they might need (Include addresses and maps.)
- A list of **local restaurants** where they might like to eat (Include addresses and maps.)
- A list of **local attractions** that they might like to see while in your area (and you could even include brochures)
- **Information on accessing public transportation** in your area, should they need to use it
- Information about a **local post office** or package shipping center

Think about including coupons or gift cards to some of the places mentioned in the packet. When preparing the packet, consider the time your missionary will have in your location. If they are only staying for a three-day mission event, the likelihood that they will utilize tickets to a local attraction are slim. On the other hand, if they are moving to your city for a six-month home assignment, they would be more likely to appreciate something like that.

If you are able, include a personal touch by handwriting a quick note in the packet. Draw their attention to local things you would highly recommend.

SECTION TWO

* * *

Prayer

*"And so, from the day we heard,
we have not ceased to pray for you,
asking that you may be filled with the
knowledge of his will in all spiritual
wisdom and understanding,"*
Colossians 1:9-12

HOW TO BLESS A MISSIONARY

PRAY FOR THEM

Although it may sound simple, one of the best ways to bless a missionary is to pray for them. There are many areas for which missionaries would appreciate prayer:

- **Effective Ministry** – Obviously, every missionary would like for their ministry to be effective and reach many people. They feel called to serve and have a passion for people coming to know God on a personal level. If their ministry is effective, it makes it easier for them to persevere in the work God gave them. They need wisdom to know when to share about Jesus and with whom.

- **Safety** – Missionaries serve in all different environments. Some live in relative safety, but others are constantly on the defensive, watching for threats. Some fear for their lives or their possessions, and others just worry about sickness and lack of medical care. Missionaries travel extensively, whether to reach their host country or to raise support in their country of origin. Many times, Americans are targets in other countries because they are perceived as rich and privileged...or just because they are Americans.

- **Strength/Stamina** – Missionaries do hard, frustrating work. Daily activities are more complicated and difficult than in the United States. Things like cooking, laundry, and housekeeping all take extra time and effort. Houses are not airtight, and bugs and dust are pervasive. People are spiritually blinded and may not be open to hearing about God. Some missionaries spend years teaching people about Jesus with no obvious progress, and no one chooses to trust in him as Savior. Pray for both physical and emotional strength.

- **Grow in Faith** – Missionaries may not have opportunities to be spiritually fed. Many live in a desert-like spiritual environment where they serve as the only well with water for those around them. Pray they receive encouragement from God's Word.

- **Personal Friendships** – Missionary life can be lonely. Working with people of another culture is hard and they may not ever be able to establish close friendships, especially if there are no Christians in their area. Their friends back in their "home" country are moving on with life without them and their relationships will never be the same. Feelings of loneliness and despair can develop quickly and unexpectedly, especially after the excitement of serving in a new place wears off.

- **Kids** – Most missionaries worry about their kids adjusting well. They want their kids to grow up healthy and emotionally stable. We must pray that the missionary parents do not become so involved in ministry that they neglect their children and family – which is their primary ministry. The list of things to pray for the MK is extensive and you can find more ideas in the next chapter.

- **Strong Marriage** – Missionaries will face many adversities that will be a trial for even the strongest marriage. We must pray for God to help them to communicate effectively and love each other unconditionally.

- **Health** – Medical care in other countries is always different than the United States. Many developing countries suffer from a lack of doctors and hospitals. There are also many snakes, bugs, and diseases that are new and dangerous to the missionary family. Even if a missionary is in a developed country, healthcare will still be different. They may have to wait on government appointments, and certain treatments and drugs may not be available.

- **Host Country Government** – Pray that the host country government would stay open to missionaries and the gospel. Pray that they make laws that facilitate people coming to know God in their country. Pray that the missionary would meet and befriend the right contacts within the local government and that they might come to know Jesus as their Savior.

- **Language Acquisition** – Learning another language (or several) can be challenging and difficult. Learning it well enough to convey emotional and spiritual truths can be even more frustrating. Some missionaries will have a natural ability to learn languages easily, while others will struggle for years and never master the local language. Pray that they can convey God's truths effectively despite a language barrier.

- **Relationships with Other Missionaries** - Relationships with other missionaries can be a very stressful part of being on the mission field. People who would have never been friends in other circumstances are thrust together and expected to work in harmony to achieve a common goal. They may come from differing denominations or they may have different personalities that do not work well together. The missionary may not feel free to discuss this or ask for prayer, but this may be a huge factor in the psychological well-being of the missionary family (including wives and children).

- **Financial Needs** – Pray that the missionary can raise enough support and have enough money to consistently meet their monthly expenses and supply their needs. Also, pray for added blessings to provide for the extra "wants" that they may have. Pray that churches and individuals would understand their ministry and want to partner with them in this way.

Want to be an even bigger blessing? Tell your missionary what you are praying for them. Write out a prayer that they can read. Let them know your thoughts and prayers, and include it in an email or handwritten note! This would be a huge encouragement for them!

PRAY FOR THEIR KIDS

You might be thinking, "Didn't we just have a chapter on praying for a missionary?". And yes, we did. But praying for a missionary's kids can require a little bit of a different focus. So, in this chapter we are going to talk about specific prayer needs of missionary kids.

- **Adjustment to New Situations** – Missionary kids are exposed to many new situations, both in their host country abroad and when they come back to their parent's passport country. Moving frequently is the norm for many of these kids. Some adjust very easily, but some struggle with each change. Prayer for easy transitions is important.

- **Language Acquisition** – Some languages are easy to pick up and learn, while others are very difficult. Some children learn languages quickly, while others seem to struggle. Younger children tend to pick up languages more easily and seem to have a better "local" accent. Pray that they learn the language quickly.

- **Salvation** – This should be the most important thing that we pray for…and the most important for the missionary parents to desire.

- **Health** – We need to pray for general medical health. They need protection from illnesses and injuries. Many children also have learning or physical disabilities, and we should pray that God would provide the appropriate medical care, therapies, and help for them and their parents. Care for things like speech problems, autism, anxiety, depression, and dyslexia are unheard of in many areas overseas. Pray for the parents to have wisdom to seek out the care needed.

- **Safety** – Missionary kids can be exposed to many different safety hazards. They may travel more often than other kids. There may be people around them that are anti-Americans or jealous of their family and would like to harm them. There may be wild animals like hippos, spiders, and snakes that could cause them harm. They may live in a village with difficult terrain that makes them more prone to broken bones and falls. Pray for God to watch over them and keep them safe.

- **Schooling** – Choosing how to educate their children is one of the biggest decisions that a missionary family will make, and it may affect where they choose to carry out their ministry. They may choose to homeschool their children, have them attend a local school, or send their child to a boarding school. Each of these choices will require a different way of praying, but we should pray that the child is able to learn well in any circumstance and that the Lord will give the parents wisdom and discernment in deciding where each child will receive education. It may be necessary for different children in the same family to receive their education in different ways.

- **Friendships** – Missionary kids need prayer to make friends, but not just any friends. They need to make the right friends. When they are little, they need good friends to play with. As they get older, they need friends that will not influence them wrongly. We should pray that they do not choose to follow pagan or evil, local practices and religions. Pray that their friends would help their faith grow and not lead them astray.
- **Identity** – Pray that the missionary kid will learn that their worth and identity are in Christ. Pray that they can identify with their parents and feel comfortable sharing concerns with them.

Send a note and let your missionary know what you are praying for their kids! Don't forget to include a note to the missionary kid telling them that you are praying for them. Mention some of the requests that you have prayed for, and give them some encouragement!

PRAY FOR THEIR MINISTRY

Every missionary wants their ministry to be effective. After all, this is why they went to the mission field in the first place. They want to reach people with the Good News about God's love and salvation. We can play a role in helping them by praying for their ministry.

- **Pray for Wisdom.** The missionary needs to have wisdom and discernment about when and where to share the gospel. They also need to have God's help in making decisions about their ministry. They may be trying to decide about a move, a ministry change, a challenging relationship, or just about whom to share the gospel with. In some countries, the missionary's life can be in danger if the Gospel or a Bible is shared with the wrong person. Pray for wisdom in their ministry decisions.

- **Pray for Receptive Hearts.** Only God can prepare someone's heart to receive and understand his gift of salvation. We can pray that God will work in the people's hearts and prepare them for what they will hear and witness through the testimony of the missionary.

- **Pray for Encouragement.** Missionaries may struggle to see any fruit from their efforts. They may work for years in a dry and barren spiritual environment without seeing even one person come to a saving faith in Jesus. We can pray that God will provide encouragement for them through His work in their lives and through other people that they encounter.

- **Pray for Safety.** Missionaries will face perils while doing their ministry. We can pray for their physical, emotional, and spiritual safety. God can give protection against Satan's attacks, and He can help the missionary have discernment about unsafe situations.

- **Pray for "Unblinded Eyes".** We must pray that God helps those that are living in blindness to his truths. We must pray for them to be able to see clearly the truth of his grace and salvation.

- **Pray for the Government.** We can pray that the missionary is allowed to remain in the country where they serve. Asking God to enable laws to be passed that facilitate missionary service is helpful. Pray for the government officials – that they would be open to hearing the gospel and letting it be spread amongst the people.

- **Pray for Infrastructure.** Many countries have sporadic electricity and water supplies. Some struggle to provide quality internet connections that are available at all times. The missionary's ministry may be hampered by reduced working hours due to lack of local infrastructure. We can pray that they have adequate electricity, water, and internet/phone service.

- **Pray for their Ability to Reach Difficult Areas.** Some missionaries are working with unreached people groups that require days of travel on foot or dependency on boats, airplanes, or canoes to arrive. We can pray that they are able to actually reach the people despite the difficulties in travel.

- **Pray for Technology.** Missionaries today use technology to help teach others about Jesus. We can pray that their devices work well and are not stolen. We can also pray that they would use their computers, tablets, phones, etc. in wise ways and in ways that local people will understand. Some missionaries may need technological items to help in their ministry and we can pray for them to receive these or find the funds to purchase them.

- **Pray for the Missionary's Spiritual Well-Being.** If a missionary is in a spiritual battle or desert, his or her ministry will not be as effective. We must pray for spiritual refreshment for them and for God to provide for their spiritual needs. We can pray that they have study time in the Bible, and that they will be able to discern the meaning of what they are studying. We can also pray that God would make Himself real in their lives and that they would sense His presence.

- **Pray for Partners.** We can pray for co-workers for the missionary (if needed). Pray that personal opinions and preferences do not get in the way of team members working together to further the gospel. Pray also for partners to come alongside them in prayer and financial support to meet the missionary's needs.

SECTION THREE

* * *

Care for Their Family

*"And let us not grow weary of doing good,
for in due season we will reap, if we do not
give up. So then, as we have opportunity,
let us do good to everyone,
and especially to those
who are of the household of faith."*
Galatians 6: 9-10

CARE FOR THEIR MISSIONARY KID

A s a former Missionary Kid (MK), I can testify that this is one way that you can be a huge blessing to a missionary family. Missionaries have limited budgets, and the money they receive is frequently allocated to ministry needs and not so much towards things they want. Many missionary kids don't have the same resources as kids living in the United States.

Here are some **practical ways to bless a missionary kid** when they are back in their parent's passport country:

- **Give them a gift**. You can send one through the mail or buy one for them and give it when they are visiting. Ask their parents ahead of time for this to be a gift tailored to something they need or want.
- Give them some **spending money**. They probably have a list (or at least a few things) that they'd really like but can't afford.
- **Take them out to eat**. Listen to them and get to know them personally. If you and their parents are comfortable, this could be just with the older child or

adolescent. You could also include other similarly aged kids from your church or community in the meal.

- Encourage your kids to **include them in parties, youth events**, etc.
- Ask them on a **play date** if they are young.
- **Offer to attend Sunday School or youth group with them**. It is very intimidating to walk into a big group of kids and be the new, "weird" missionary kid. Even if they are back at their "home church", it won't be home for them and they will be uncomfortable. If they know you, you can help ease this transition.
- **Sponsor them** so they are able to go to a church camp.
- **Give them a job**. Missionary kids are usually not able to have a "normal" job. Most of the time there are rules against them working in the country where their parents work due to legal issues with paperwork. Then, they are in their parent's passport country infrequently and may not be able to be hired for a normal job due to their travel schedules. If you have temporary work they can do to earn some pay, they would probably appreciate it very much.
- **Host them** if their parents are out of the country and they do not have a place to stay. This can be short-term (days or weeks) or long-term (months or years).
- **Write them a note of encouragement.**
- **Write a letter of recommendation for them** if they are trying to obtain admission or scholarships for college. (This requires for you to know them.)

- **Buy them a gift when they graduate from high school.**
- **Throw them a "Going to College" shower.** They may only have 1-2 suitcases of clothes to take to college, and the needs may be great. You can help provide sheets, pillows, a desk lamp, a fan, school supplies, etc. This can be a surprise, or you can ask the family what the MK's specific needs are. You could even provide a gift card shower so the MK and their parents can go shopping and get what they need.
- **Invite the Missionary Kid in college for lunch after church.** They don't have family close, and it can be very lonely to leave a church service and head back to an empty dorm room or cafeteria alone. Even if the MK has friends, it can be a blessing to have an older person take an interest in them and be available for advice and encouragement.
- **Invite them for holidays like Thanksgiving and Christmas.** Most dorms are closed and empty over certain holidays. Giving the missionary kid a place to stay and a family to celebrate with can be a blessing.

I was blessed to have people do several of the above things for me. I had a "Going to College" shower that was a huge blessing, both to me and my parents. My parents wanted to provide for all the things I might need before they left me and drove thousands of miles away, but they did not have the budget for it. Our sending church sponsored a shower for me, and I was able to go to the dorm with all of the basics that I would need for my freshman year. It was a big relief!

I also had a few people that gave me money over the years to spend on things I might want or need. One man wrote a letter of recommendation to help me get a scholarship for college. One sweet lady took me out to lunch (by myself) several times. Our family knew her, and approved, of course. It made me feel very special that she would invest in me by spending time with me!

I received several notes of encouragement during my university years from ladies from my sending church that knew our family. It was nice to learn of news from our church, as well as hear some encouraging words. Receiving a letter in my mailbox was special because I rarely received one.

I was also able to stay with a family for a few weeks after I moved out of the university dorm for summer vacation. My parents were returning to the U.S.A. and I was going to join them, but I did not have a place to stay for those few weeks until they arrived.

I hope you have been inspired to think outside of the box today! How can you bless a Missionary Kid?

CARE FOR THEIR ELDERLY OR ILL FAMILY MEMBER

Overseas workers, just like us, have family members that get sick or need extra care from time to time. The difference is that they are not always able to be present to care for them. Many missionaries struggle with being far away from an ill family member when they are sick.

Some have elderly parents that are not acutely ill but need some extra help with specific activities. They may have Alzheimer's disease, a broken hip, or be recovering from knee replacement surgery. They may also just be growing older and becoming unable to complete their daily activities. I have known missionaries who were forced to return home from their ministry because someone was not available to care for their family member, and the responsibility fell on them.

So, an out-of-the-box way that you can be a blessing to a missionary is to offer to care for their family member. Examples of family members that may need extra care include:

- Elderly parents
- Sick parents, siblings, or children
- Missionary kids that have returned for school in the United States, their parent's passport country, or are at boarding school

Ways that you can be helpful might include such things as:
- Taking them to doctor appointments or physical therapy
- Sitting with them in the hospital
- Reading to them
- Helping them write letters or emails
- Driving them to church, Bible studies, or book clubs
- Making meals to take to them or inviting them over for a meal
- Going grocery shopping for them
- Cleaning their house
- Mowing their lawn or doing yard work
- Respite care (sitting with an ill person while the primary caretaker gets a break)
- Giving a care package
- Writing notes of encouragement
- Providing a home for the MK to live in while going to college

Organize a group of people from your church that will take turns doing some of these simple jobs or ask people to sign up for one thing. With more people involved, the burden of care is spread among many people and each person will have a chance to be a blessing and bless someone else.

A great way to be an encouragement to the missionary is to send them an email or call them on the phone to give them an update about their family member. You might even include some photos so they can see their family. They will feel relieved and grateful to know that their loved one is being checked on and looked out for.

HOW TO BLESS A MISSIONARY

PROVIDE CHILDCARE FOR THEM

This area of blessing is one that is frequently overlooked, but can be a big help to your missionary. You (and your church) can provide childcare for a missionary that needs it. Reasons the missionary might need childcare include:

- Doctor visits
- Teaching or training conference
- Missionary conference
- Counseling sessions
- Missionary retreat
- Marriage retreat or conference
- Car shopping
- Packing
- Cleaning
- To allow them to care for another family member

As you can see, missionaries face some of the same challenges that most parents do. If you know the missionary well, they might be fine with you watching the children in your home or caring for them overnight. Make sure you know about any allergies, likes, and dislikes the children might have. Also, discuss pets and potential childhood fears with the parents. Always have a way to contact the parents.

Churches can also provide a safe place for children to be watched and cared for during the daytime hours. Think about whether your church has the budget to pay childcare workers for this or whether you will need volunteers. Offer this at different times when the missionary is in your community. They should not feel that they have to use funds that people have donated to pay for someone to watch their child. You can help them be a good steward of their resources in this way.

SPONSOR AN EVENT FOR MISSIONARY WIVES

The missionary wife is often the glue that holds the missionary family together. Looking for special ways to bless her will help her continue and persevere in the role that God has given her.

The missionary wife can face many different pressures. In the country where her family lives and serves, she will likely have increased physical and psychological pressures every day. Cleaning, cooking, shopping, and housekeeping can be very difficult in another country. Depending on where she lives, she may not have clean water (or any water), electricity, or she may have to grow and cultivate her own food. Even if she lives in a large city, she will likely spend hours shopping for groceries and cleaning and preparing food so that it is ready to be used.

Some missionary wives have a ministry outside the home, but many have a full-time job just maintaining the family home and raising children. For those with a ministry with the local people, language barriers and cultural differences can make their activities very difficult and stressful. Preparing to speak and pray in a language that one does speak proficiently is very hard.

For the wives and moms that primarily care for the home and family, isolation and loneliness can be a constant companion. Living in a different culture and speaking an Americanized version of the local language can wreak havoc on that mom and wife's mental well-being. She may feel inadequate and constantly long for the familiarity and ease of living back in her passport country.

This is where you come in! Churches, small groups, and individuals can host an event to benefit the missionary wives. Here are some examples you can try:

1. **A Large Event for Missionary Wives at your church** – Your church can plan an evening, a day, or a weekend to bless these ladies. Invite all those involved in your missions conference, as well as those that are supported by your church. Make this an annual or biannual event. Consider inviting special speakers that can bless the ladies (don't ask the missionary wives to speak). Sponsor special activities like a tea party, a manicure, a craft, a visit to get a makeover at a local salon, and have a quiet prayer room with candles, soft music, and chairs, pillows, or benches. Arrange childcare for those that will need it.

2. **A Gathering for the Missionary Wife to Share About Her Life** – This can be large or small and include any number of people. Ask the ladies of your local church to attend a lunch, brunch, or dinner in her honor and ask her to share about her ministry and family. Give her some questions ahead of time or ask them in person. Give her a gift that will make her feel valued and appreciated.

3. **A Gathering in Another Country to Honor Local Missionary Wives** – This idea will require a little more coordination and planning, but it can be a huge blessing. My mom experienced this one time during my parent's many years of ministry. A church group from the United States coordinated and hosted a retreat for missionary wives in Central Mexico. They found a retreat location that had "cabins" and different bunkbeds for the ladies to sleep in. The ladies were treated to a Friday night and Saturday full of events and spiritual nourishment. Ladies came from all over Mexico to attend this event and were blessed. The events that the host group planned included Bible study, crafts (they brought the supplies), a tea party (they brought fancy tea cups to use and send home with each missionary wife), and chances for sports/exercise. They also cooked and provided the food for the event.

4. **A Lunch "Date"** – This can be something simple to pull off. Check with the missionary wife and ask if you could meet for a meal together during their time in their country of origin. You can meet one-on-one, or you can include a group of ladies from your small group or church. Celebrating a birthday or anniversary with her is special, too.

Consider if one of these is something you would be able to plan. It will be a blessing to both the missionary wife and her family!

SPONSOR AN EVENT FOR MISSIONARY KIDS

Missionary kids are under tremendous amounts of pressure and stress. They live in a different culture and are surrounded by people that speak differently than them. Many times, they do not look like the people that they live around. They are a subset of third-culture kids (TCKs), made of their own distinct mix of formative cultures.

Now, add to the above stresses the constant watchful eye of hundreds of supporters, each with their own opinion about how the missionary kid should act, dress, and where they should go to school. It can be overwhelming and very discouraging!

Many missionary kids do not identify with the culture they live in, and they do not feel any connection to their parents' home culture. They do not belong anywhere. They will likely continue to feel like they do not fit in anywhere for the rest of their lives. (Some are more resilient and will go on to become high achievers, but others will struggle with this for years to come.)

You can be a blessing to a missionary kid! You and your church or small group can plan an event that will make the MK feel valued and loved. Here are some ideas to get you started:

1. **A Large Gathering for Missionary Kids at Your Church** – You can organize a conference or retreat for MKs at or near your local church. Invite special speakers that specialize in MK issues or a Christian psychologist that knows about trauma and transitions. Plan special activities, depending on the age of the kids. Smaller kids will love a VBS-type environment, while older MKs will enjoy some sessions with information, crafts, sports, and other activities.

2. **A Small Gathering for the Missionary Kid to Attend** – This can be as simple as including them in the youth activities or planning a special movie or sport activity in their honor. The intent of this activity should be to help others get to know them, while helping them feel welcomed and included.

3. **A Retreat for Missionary Kids in the Country Where They Live** – This will require more planning and volunteers, but can be a huge blessing. Plan a time where MKs can go to an overnight or day camp and spend time with other MKs. Look for people experienced in MK issues and psychology to help out. Organize activities like crafts, sports, etc. You could even form teams to help with team-building exercises, form bonds, and increase the feeling of inclusion.

Just a note: Most MKs will not think that an event is fun if it is only focused on them. They do not usually love being in the spotlight, and making them speak, answer questions, or perform music will not bless them. (I am generalizing, but most MKs are expected to do these things on a regular basis. Many wish they did not have to do these things.) The idea should be to provide a place where they can rest or hang out as one of a group of kids – not to single them out for entertainment or educational purposes.

Think about how much you can bless a missionary family by blessing their MK. Decide if your church can plan an event for MKs. Include the older MKs that are now grown-ups in your community. Offering some perspective from someone who has "been there and done that" or who truly can understand where they are coming from can be invaluable.

SECTION FOUR

* * *

Help Them Raise Support

"And God is able to make all grace abound to you,
so that having all sufficiency in all things at all times,
you may abound in every good work."
2 Corinthians 9:8

ADVOCATE FOR YOUR CHURCH TO HOST THEM

Missionaries visit many churches when they are back in the United States (or other countries of origin) on home assignment. Some organizations help set up church visits, but many missionaries must arrange their own visits to churches during their time in the U.S.A. With so many missionaries in existence and a finite amount of churches and money available, it can be challenging for a missionary to get an appointment to talk with a missions committee or present their ministry in a church.

This is where you come in! A pastor is more likely to schedule a time to talk to a missionary or have them present their ministry to his church when he knows that some people in his local congregation know the missionary and believe in their ministry. Personal connections go a long way!

What can you do?

- Find out when your missionary will be on "home assignment" or "furlough".

- Find out from your missionary if they would like to come to your church or if they would like you to ask about it.
- Find out when your church has a "Missions Sunday", missions conference or if they allow missionaries to present at other times.
- If you are the pastor of your church, promote the missionary to your staff and plan a time for them to visit.
- If you are not the pastor, approach your Missions Pastor or Lead Pastor with a proposal to have the missionary come. Be prepared to discuss your missionary with them and promote them. They might agree to a meeting with the pastor, a presentation in a Sunday School class, or a presentation from the pulpit. You never know!
- Have your missionary's contact information available.
- If a meeting time is not possible, ask your pastor if your church provides for missionaries needs. Be prepared with one or two specific needs your missionary will have while on home assignment.

While this may seem like a waste of time to some or pointless to others, you would be surprised how much this can help! My family was able to visit many churches because of a local connection. Although not all of them were able to support us financially each month, some gave a one-time financial gift, and some joined as prayer partners. This was invaluable to my parent's ministry.

Can you contact your local church leadership and advocate for a missionary? I challenge you to give it a try!

ORGANIZE A DINNER FOR THEM AT YOUR CHURCH

Recently, one of our church's missionaries was back in the United States for a visit. A lunch meeting was planned, and the church needed volunteers to buy and prepare food for a meal after the morning services. Our missionaries were going to share their story, ministry, and vision with anyone attending the lunch meeting.

A simple way that we were able to help was to purchase supplies for the lunch. We decided on a "make-your-own-deli-sandwich" buffet. This only required a little bit of time to go to the store, set the supplies up on trays, and make sure that the food was ready. Those attending were able to eat sandwiches, fruit, chips, and cookies…and they were able to get to know the missionaries better.

Another option would be to plan and organize a potluck for your church family before or after the church service when the missionary will be there. It can be a breakfast option, full meal, or just something as simple as an ice cream social. The idea is to let the missionary share more in depth and afford the people of the church the opportunity to get to know them better.

When I was growing up, I remember one church in particular that hosted a church-wide potluck after the Sunday morning service each time that we visited. I still remember the kindness of the people and watching my parents visit with many people over a meal. Although there was no formal presentation at these meals, we grew to know some of the church people through these meals over the years.

Because of the lunch we attended at our own church, we are more informed about what things to pray for. We learned specific needs. We now know what their kids look like. Our memory will hopefully be triggered, and we will think of them when we see certain things. Our kids were able to listen to them and will remember meeting them and hearing about where they work.

I would encourage you to look for opportunities like this! Your kids will talk about it for days.

OFFER TO HELP THEM RAISE SUPPORT

O ne of the least favorite tasks of many missionaries is raising support. If you are not familiar with this term, it means asking people to donate money to their ministry. Mission organizations typically help missionaries know how much money they will need to have from donors on a monthly basis. Some mission organizations then provide this amount once the missionary has been approved, but most organizations require that the missionary asks people to donate to supply the funds.

Missionaries can raise support from different sources:
- Individuals
- Churches
- Sunday School Classes
- Small Groups
- Organizations
- Businesses

Some people choose to give a one-time donation or offering. Some will commit to give a monthly amount. Giving online makes this much easier now because people can schedule a credit card payment every month or a monthly withdrawal from their bank account. A bonus is that donations are usually tax-deductible.

So, **how can you help raise support for a missionary**? Here are several ideas:

1. First, **become an expert about your missionary**. You need to know what their ministry is and how they go about achieving it. If you are going to be promoting them, you need to be able to answer a reasonable amount of questions about them. Make sure you know any websites and blog addresses. Know how people can donate.

2. **Talk about your missionary with your friends**. Ask your friends if they have ever considered supporting a missionary and encourage them to pray about it. Share your own experience of giving. Explain that the amount they give does not have to be huge – maybe they can start with $10 or $25 dollars per month.

3. **Propose that your Sunday School class or small group consider donating** a monthly amount or at least a one-time donation. You can adopt a missionary family and follow their ministry together.

4. **Ask your church to support your missionary**. If your missionary is not currently receiving support from your church, ask your pastor to consider "taking them on" as part of the missionary support that your church donates on a

monthly basis. The amount can be as small as $25 per month but can also be much higher.

5. **Offer to help them take a family picture for their "prayer card" or website**. Or better yet, if you have experience, help them design a "prayer card". Most missionaries have some kind of postcard or greeting card with their picture. They give these out to people and churches to help people remember to pray for them and to ask for support.

6. **Pay for postage for the missionary to send requests for support.** Many requests are sent via email now, but a certain number of requests for more financial support will still be sent via regular mail. This is something that a local church or an individual can help with. You could even offer to print letters, stuff envelopes, and apply address labels for the missionary's letters.

Take a moment and consider how you can help a missionary raise support! Asking people for money is never comfortable. Just think how often they have to present their financial needs to others, and then realize what a blessing you can be in helping to help alleviate some of that load. They will appreciate your help!

SPONSOR A MISSIONS CONFERENCE AT YOUR CHURCH

Hosting a missions conference is one of the most traditional ways that churches have sought to help missionaries share their ministry. These conferences or events can last anywhere from one day to a month. Churches can be very instrumental in facilitating a meeting between a missionary and the people that need to hear about their ministry.

Each church will need to decide the amount of time, manpower, money, and resources they have to dedicate to this. Here are some ideas of things you can choose to include in your missionary conference:

- Missionary speakers to share the sermon
- Missionary speakers to give updates on their ministry from the pulpit
- Missionary speakers to speak in Sunday Schools
- Missionary speakers to speak in children's events

- Missionary wives to speak at a women's event
- Bilingual/foreign language songs or hymns of worship during the services
- Songs about evangelism and spreading the news about salvation, songs about the nations praising together
- A parade of flags during the opening/closing service
- Flags hanging around the sanctuary
- Slideshows of missionary pictures playing before and after services
- A map of the world with missionary pictures to show where they work
- A prayer meeting with specific missions related prayer requests
- Missionary information tables/displays where missionaries can show others about their ministry
- Prayer cards for each missionary that members of the congregation take and make a commitment to pray
- A church dinner – can be catered or potluck with foods from around the world
- A "Trip Around the World" – a different room for each missionary to decorate or display items. They can do a slide show or just explain their ministry. Groups of church members rotate through the different rooms at determined time intervals (20 minutes, for example) and get to hear about several different ministries in greater detail. For more fun, you can make passports that they will get stamped in each room.

- A list or table showcasing books related to missions that the congregation might be interested in (including children's books)
- Children's sessions that help children "travel" to different places or understand different types of mission work
- A special offering for the missionaries attending the conference or for a specific need of a certain missionary or project
- A special project that the congregation can work together to complete (compiling a newly translated and printed Bible in another language, collecting maternity items for the local pregnancy crisis center, collecting items for the homeless shelter, cleaning a local ministry location)
- A shopping event to take the missionaries attending the conference to buy something new
- Missionary visits to the Missions Closet (this idea is explained in another chapter)
- A visit to a local spa to receive a makeover or massage for the missionary wives
- A welcome packet with information about your church and city
- A special gift for each missionary family attending the event (money and tangible gifts are both nice)
- Specific Sunday School classes can adopt different missionary families (for the conference or long-term)

Use your imagination and put together a team of people that can help plan and organize a conference for your church. If you have never had a conference, start small and include only a few missionary families. Try only a few of the included items in the list when you are beginning a new tradition, but add to it each year. Your church members will grow to love the conference and the closeness to the missionaries that it brings.

SECTION FIVE

* * *

Provide for Their Needs

*"And you Philippians yourselves know that in the
beginning of the gospel, when I left Macedonia,
no church entered into partnership with me in
giving and receiving, except you only.
Even in Thessalonica you sent me help for my
needs once and again.
Not that I seek the gift, but I seek the fruit that
increases to your credit.
I have received full payment, and more. I am
well supplied, having received from Epaphroditus
the gifts you sent, a fragrant offering,
a sacrifice acceptable and pleasing to God.
And my God will supply every need of yours
according to his riches in glory in Christ Jesus."
Philippians 4:15-19*

DONATE SERVICES

Many churches and people would love to help a missionary, but do not have extra cash lying around to donate. One practical way that you can help a missionary is to donate services to them. Maybe you own a small business or maybe you have a particular skill that can be useful to them. You might have members of your church that have the skills necessary to help. Even if you cannot donate the entire amount of a service, you might have a coupon for a particular service that would help them out a lot.

Here are some practical examples of ways you might help; use your imagination to come up with other ways that fit your skills and talents!

- **Donate services for their car**. Maybe they need an oil change or new tires. Maybe they need new brakes. Offer a discount if you have a car repair shop. Give them a free car wash or a free set of tires.
- **Offer to cut and color their hair**. This is an expensive item that many missionaries do not treat themselves to regularly. If you know how to do this well, you can make

them feel very pampered. (Just don't walk up and say, "I can color your hair for you!" That might not be received well.)

- **Donate airfare miles**. Many people that travel a lot have these stored up. The missionary could use these to travel to churches while on furlough or to help pay for a return ticket home. Maybe you work for an airline and can donate a buddy pass to them, or maybe you travel extensively for work and never use your miles/points.

- **Offer to help fix their computer**. Missionaries have "I.T." problems just like the rest of us. If you are experienced with computers, you can be a huge help to a missionary with limited funds.

- **Work on their website or blog**. If you know how to write code or design a website, this can be extremely helpful. Maybe you know how to do graphic design or make images they can use to promote their ministry.

- **Do yardwork for them** for free while they are on home assignment. This can be a huge timesaver and blessing to the missionary. This is also a great way to get your kids or youth group involved.

- **Take pictures of them**. If you can take professional quality pictures, your missionary would probably love to have some new, beautiful pictures of their family. They may need one to update their prayer card, newsletter, or blog.

- **Offer free copies**. If you happen to own a copy/print store, you can offer to make free copies of newsletters for them. Many churches might also be able to offer this service.

- **Donate food**. Do you own a restaurant, café, or food business? Treat them to a meal or two. Depending on the establishment, you could donate coffee, donuts, bread, meals, ice cream, cakes, or cookies. Maybe you can supply milk to a growing family from your local farm or let them pick their own fruit for free.

- **Share your garden produce**. If you've spent time and effort cultivating a garden in the summer, you probably have an abundance of produce. Ask the missionary if they would like some fresh garden food. Missionaries travel a lot, so it is a good idea to make sure they will be in town to be able to eat it. Most missionaries will probably be very appreciative of some freshly grown food.

- **Do alterations**. If you are a skilled seamstress or tailor or own an alteration shop, you can help a missionary alter clothing or hem pants.

- **Tutor their kids**. If you are a teacher, you could be very useful by tutoring their kids. Many MKs struggle to adjust during their time on "home assignment" and a tutor may be immensely helpful.

- **Babysit**. Offer to watch the MKs for a date night or for the parents to be able to attend a doctor's appointment, etc. This can be a great way to involve your teenage kids in ministry.

- **Do physicals for free or reduced cost**. Are you a physician, physician's assistant, or nurse practitioner?

Depending on your practice's rules, you may be able to do check-ups for the missionary or their children at reduced or no cost. You also might be able to provide samples of medication for them to use.

- **Offer lessons.** If you are a teacher of a musical instrument or style of art, you can offer lessons for free or at a reduced cost. The missionary or their children might love to take violin lessons or learn to paint with acrylic paint on a canvas.

- **Offer financial planning or tax help.** If you are a CPA or experienced with financial investments, you can be a huge help to a missionary. They may need help completing their taxes each year, and the rules may be different for them depending on whether or not they have foreign-earned income. You can also help them know about options for saving money for retirement, investing, and saving for college. Most missionaries are not educated about these things, and they probably don't have extra time to spend trying to learn about them.

Depending on your skills and talents and what business you might own, you might be able to come up with even more ways to donate services to a missionary. Maybe you can come up with one that I did not think of!

SEND A PACKAGE TO THEM

O ne of the most old-fashioned ways to bless a missionary is to send a package to them. In order to do this well, it is probably best to first ask the missionary if it is ok for them to receive packages. They will be able to tell you any information that you might need to send the package in the best way possible.

You will need to know:
- What can or cannot be sent to them
- How best to send it (Fed Ex, UPS, USPS, etc.)
- Any fees they may have to pay to get the package out of customs
- If it can contain anything regarding God, Jesus, or Christianity
- What they may need or want.
- If things are stolen and they never receive packages that have been sent to them.

There are a few things that are NOT good things to send. **Do NOT send**:

- **Used clothing** in outdated or poor condition. If you wouldn't wear it, don't send it. (Of course, if the missionary has requested this, you may send it.)
- **Baked goods and popped popcorn** (unless specifically requested). You do not know how long the package will be in transit, and the food may be stale or in crumbs by the time the missionary gets it. This is also an invitation for bugs to invade the packaging.
- **Old tea bags, coffee grounds, and partially used things.** Believe it or not, missionaries receive things like this from well-meaning people. Not only is this an insult, but the missionary will likely have to pay to get these out of customs and then will have no use for them.
- **Old and outdated books and commentaries** (unless the missionary knows about them and wants them). These are heavy and hard to ship. If the missionary must pay to get things out of customs, they may have to pay more than they are worth.
- **Outdated media**. Those old VHS tapes, cassette tapes, and CD's that you don't want…they don't want them either. (And they may not have a way to even play them!)

The moral of the story is this: you can bless a missionary with a package but check with them first! They will be excited to receive things that they cannot purchase in the country where they serve or things that they have been wishing for!

HOST THEM IN YOUR HOME

O ne way that we have chosen to bless missionaries is to host them in our home. This also has proven to have an added benefit – our kids see the missionaries and get to know them and their children, even if only for an evening. We have been able to host several missionaries for dinners and lunches in our home. This is a great way for a whole family to be involved, and it doesn't have to cost a ton of money if your family happens to be on a tight budget.

So, how do you do this if you don't know any missionaries or don't know when they will be in town?

One option is to contact your local pastor and find out what missionaries will be coming through your area. Have your church put you on a list to be contacted when missionaries will be coming. Let them know what you are willing to provide.

You can also find out when a missionary that you have befriended might be coming through. We had started following the newsletters from, and had written several emails to, a family in Brazil. We soon found out that they would be coming to the United States and we offered to feed them or have them stay with us if they were in our area. The first time we met them in person, they ended up driving through for supper on their way to another destination. We might not have ever met them if we had not contacted them and invited them to come. On a later visit, they were able to eat supper and stay the night in our home.

When I was growing up, my family benefited from staying with many different people. We had people in different states and cities that we got to know because we ate or stayed in their home. This was a big blessing to us because we did not have extra money to pay for frequent hotels during our travels. We had many people that hosted us for meals, but we also stayed overnight with many people while travelling. We even stayed for several weeks one summer in the basement of a family that offered to let us use it. I also benefited from a family that let me stay with them for 2 weeks one summer until my parents came back to visit churches that summer.

If your church can afford to maintain a home that can be used for hosting visiting missionaries visit, that can be a huge blessing! Being able to rest and regroup in their "own space" for a few days or weeks can help them immensely. We benefited from a local church that maintained a "Mission House" where their visiting missionaries could stay, and this is discussed in another chapter.

Here are a few things to consider in order to be a **GREAT HOST**:

- Make sure that you have a **private area** for the missionary and their children to sleep. You would think this would be obvious and not need to be said, but I'm saying it anyway. Not everyone seems to realize how important this is. You don't have to have a basement or private apartment.... a normal bedroom will do. It is just awkward if there is no way for them to close a door for privacy or if you expect their children to sleep with yours. Remember, they are strangers and may not feel comfortable with this. Probably the best scenario is if you do have a basement area where they can sleep without interruptions and where they can have their own bathroom facilities.

- **Provide clean sheets and towels**.
- **Find out about allergies**. Many people these days seem to have allergies to all sorts of different things. You'd hate to serve spaghetti and find out that they can't have gluten, prepare food with nuts when they have a life-threatening allergy, or put them in the room where the dog normally sleeps if they are allergic to dogs!
- **Prepare your Wi-Fi password**. Most missionaries are very globally interconnected. They may not have a large data plan or internet access, and they will likely be very grateful to be able to use your Wi-Fi. They may need to check emails, prepare presentations, or communicate with the next people on their journey.
- **Prepare a gift bag**. This can be anything your church or family would like and can afford. Maybe it's a collection of travel-sized toiletries for them to use while in your home and that they can take with them. Maybe it has travel activities and snacks for the kids. Maybe it has an item for a home (if they are on home assignment). Maybe

you can afford to put some gift cards in. Use your imagination and get the kids involved!

- **Safety can be a concern** in this day and age. It is sad that this has to be addressed, but you need to make sure that your own family will be safe. Make sure that you are not on the opposite end of the house from where your children and the missionaries are sleeping, or at least make sure that the doors can be locked. We always want to think the best of people that are serving the Lord in ministry, but there is always a risk that someone may have sinful tendencies that they may not be able to resist. If this is a concern for you, I suggest paying for a hotel for them. Your first responsibility is to your own family.

SEND CHRISTMAS GIFTS TO THEM

W hen is the best time to start thinking about Christmas presents for missionaries? Anytime is a great time! You might want to send a package, or you might want to donate a special amount of money for them to use in buying Christmas presents for their own family.

This is something that your church can get involved in, too. Make a list of items that you want to send to the missionary, and ask for people in the church to donate them. There might be people that only wish to donate money and others that can do the shopping. Collect the items for a few weeks and then host a wrapping/packing party. (Make sure that the gifts can be gift-wrapped in order to clear customs.)

Some people do not have a lot of extra money, and they can barely afford to buy gifts for their own family. If you are short on extra cash, you can watch for deals all year long in order to find something you can afford that will be a blessing to the missionary. Look in the clearance sections of the store – seasonal times like Christmas, Easter, and back-to-school tend to have left-over items steeply discounted. (Just remember to look for things the missionary will find exciting or useful.)

Sending a package to a missionary with Christmas presents in it is a great idea, but it requires a bit of forethought. Contact the missionary you would like to send something to and find out what they might need or like. Also, find out about how to send a package or what you may not be able to send. It may take weeks or months for them to receive it. There is another chapter in this book that deals with sending packages more specifically.

Sending money as a Christmas gift is also a great idea. This may allow the missionary to buy Christmas presents for their family that they otherwise couldn't afford. They might be able to purchase something they have been needing or wanting that wasn't in the normal budget. Find out how to send money to them– usually there is a way to make a payment online through their ministry website, but you may have to send in a check. (An added benefit for you is that sending money is usually tax-deductible.)

To make an even bigger impact, join together with your Sunday School class, homeschool group, extended family or neighbors and participate together to give an even bigger monetary gift. Your missionary may be able to purchase the washing machine, motorcycle, or car that they have been needing!

BUY A MAGAZINE SUBSCRIPTION FOR THEM

Contact your missionary friend and find out what kinds of magazines they might enjoy reading. Learn about what interests they have. What do they like?

- Parenting
- Homeschooling
- Photography
- Fishing
- Hunting
- Carpentry
- DIY
- Travel
- Aviation
- Music
- Children's interests

You'll need to find out if they prefer to read it electronically or you can check to see if they can receive the paper version in the mail. You'll also have to check with the magazine to see if they ship overseas (it might cost a little more for overseas shipping). You'll either need an email or a street/P.O. Box address. (You might check to make sure that magazine is allowed in the country they live in…some countries are closed to certain religious ideas or fashion trends.)

Look up a magazine that matches their interest and order it for them or for their children. Reading a magazine in English might help them feel a connection with the people and places they left behind. They may even enjoy reading as a family. Missionary kids usually have less access to many English reading materials.

You can do this on any budget! Many magazines are available at steep discounts at different times through the year. If you participate in a recycling program in your community, you can use reward points to order magazines for other people and it won't cost you anything!

This is a great idea for a gift that is not a one-time thing…they will keep receiving new issues throughout the whole year. (By the way, this is a great gift for anyone!)

TAKE THEM SHOPPING

Taking a missionary shopping may sound a little overwhelming, especially if you are an introvert or if you don't know them well. BUT, believe me, this can be a huge blessing!

There are two ways that I have seen this happen:

1. **Organize a shopping trip as a church** for multiple missionaries visiting at the same time. I know a church that does this every year during their missionary focus week and it works well. They assign a designated amount of money for each member of each missionary family and assign church volunteers to accompany them to the mall. It is an event for all the missionary families and church volunteers to participate in at the same time. They take pictures and then share them on Sunday with the congregation. Many times, the missionaries will buy things like tennis shoes, pants, and bathrobes. You'd be surprised how grateful they are to buy some of these things they have been needing, but unable to afford.

2. **Take them shopping individually.** If you are meeting them for lunch or hosting them in your home, you can figure out a time to take them shopping while you are with them or while they are in town.

Things to consider:

Decide ahead of time if you'd like to surprise the missionary or let them know ahead of time. It might work best to plan the time, since most missionaries have a schedule to keep when they are back in their passport country.

Remember, you don't have to go to a huge mall or shopping center. Pick a smaller store if time is short. You need to decide what you want to take them shopping for and this will help determine where you go. Are you going to let them buy whatever they want? Are you going to ask them to identify something they need? Are you going to offer to spoil them by buying an expensive perfume or makeup? Are there kids involved?

Do you need to set a budget? If you have limited funds, you need to decide ahead of time how much you are willing to spend. Letting the missionary know an idea of what you are planning will help them not to feel uncomfortable during the shopping experience. If you only have a specific amount to spend, you can let the missionary know how much or just give them the cash and let them spend it.

Have you ever taken a missionary shopping? Consider giving it a try! It can be really special to get something they would not normally get. My mom had a lady that took her to the mall and let her purchase a perfume from the perfume counter at a large department store. She could pick any one she wanted. It was a little overwhelming because she had never owned anything like that, but it was fun and she treasured that perfume (and the gesture of love that it represented).

LOAN THEM SOMETHING

H ave you ever traveled somewhere and had to rent a car when you arrived? Or have you had to figure out how to get a car seat for your child once you got there?

Many missionaries travel long distances to return to their country of origin, and then they travel again and again repeatedly while there. Most don't own cars in their passport country, and some will not have access to a car seat once they arrive.

One way you can help is to loan them something like a car or child's car seat. These things are bulky and cumbersome, and they might need them while in your area. This could save them hundreds of dollars. They might only need to use it for a weekend, a week, or they might need it for the whole summer. Find out what their needs are and see how you can help. Even if you can only help part of the time, this can still be a huge help. This also helps the missionary family be good stewards of the money they are receiving from donors. They don't need to waste donated money on a rental car if someone local can let them use one for a few days.

If you think about it, you might even be able to figure out some other things that a missionary could use. All you probably need to do is ask them. Do they need a saw, a blender, a ladder, a lawn mower? Do their kids need some bicycles while they are on home assignment? Could they use a stroller? I am sure that you could think of other ideas. Try to put yourself in their shoes and use your imagination to think what they might need. By lending something to them, you will be blessing them.

DONATE MONEY

One of the most obvious ways to be a blessing to a missionary is to donate money to their ministry. Many people choose to give to missions through their local church, and this is a great option. But did you know that you can donate money to a missionary without giving it through your local church? This can be a wonderful way to feel more involved and connected to them. (This should not take the place of your normal, regular tithing to the local church; it should be in addition to it.)

You can choose to do this in several different ways, depending on your budget:

- **One time** – Give a one-time gift when you have the money available or choose a special occasion like a birthday or Christmas. (This can bless the missionary by supplying some extra funds for something they have been needing or wanting.) If finances are tight, think about this as an option especially when tax refunds are given, when you receive a bonus from work, or when you sell a big-ticket item.

- **On a regular schedule** – monthly giving is the most common frequency, but you could choose quarterly or yearly. Giving on a regular basis is a huge blessing! This helps the missionary to plan ahead and know how much income to expect on a monthly basis. They can then budget accordingly. Most mission agencies require missionaries to raise a specific monthly amount to be able to go to the mission field.

- **Both monthly donations and special gifts** – This will bless the missionary the most. They will have a regular income to count on, but will have special times of blessing when unexpected donations come. My family had one supporter that did this. We received a recurring amount from them monthly, but every spring we would receive a special donation. The amount varied each time, as it was tied to his business income and tax refund.

How do you donate money? You have options. You can give money **directly** to a missionary that is visiting. (Doing this means you won't get a receipt for a tax-deduction, but you'll get to give it to them personally!) You could also send a **check** to their mission address or P.O. Box. Just make sure you know to whom to make out the check.

The best way, in my opinion, is to sign up for **automatic donations online** from your bank account or credit card. (This is the easiest! You won't forget to send in the money that they are counting on if it happens automatically. This is especially easy if you already have several other bills set up to be paid automatically.)

How do you find someone to send your money to?

- Ask your Missions Pastor or another church leader.
- Look up the missionaries that your church supports.
- Meet them at a missions conference.
- Ask a friend if they have a missionary that they donate to.
- Read about missionaries online and pick one. Make sure that their mission agency is a reputable one (read about their mission statement and core values, find out how they manage their money, etc.) Find a ministry that sounds interesting to you and your family. If you are really into music, find a missionary that sings or leads music classes as an outreach. If you love aviation, pick a missionary pilot or mechanic. If you know about education, pick a missionary that is teaching – whether at a missionary school or at an international school. As you can see, the possibilities are endless.

While donations from churches are very important, I can tell you, from personal experience, just how much of a difference a donation by a family can make. My parents financial support (donations of money) came from a relatively small number of churches and a large list of supporting couples and families that made it a priority to send money every month. Some sent only 10 or 25 dollars per month. This may seem like a very small amount of money in the big scheme of things, but it all added up. If it were not for these families and their faithful giving, we would have never been able to go to the mission field. You, too, can make a difference in the life of a missionary!

PROVIDE A VACATION HOME OR RV

Vacation season comes every year, and many families are making plans for trips during the warmer months. Missionaries usually have to travel quite a bit, but it is not usually for pleasure or a vacation. While in their passport country, they are tasked with traveling to different churches and visiting different supporting individuals. Their schedule can be exhausting, and staying with strangers or acquaintances can be very stressful. Sometimes, they long to "go home" to the country where they serve to be able to rest a little bit and get away from the chaos and spotlight.

You can help provide a much-needed rest in the midst of this chaos. Do you have a vacation home, timeshare, or RV? You can offer this to a visiting missionary and give them the possibility of getting away for a few days. Due to financial constraints, this may be the only way they could ever experience something like this.

Now, you may be thinking, "My timeshare isn't anywhere exotic. I don't think anyone would be interested." Even if you think it is in the middle of the United States in a "boring" location - the missionary can still get away to rest and recharge.

Make sure you know the exact dates that the home or RV is available. Also, make sure you know any rules about who can stay there or use it, and pass these on to the missionary. If the house, RV, or timeshare is far away from where you live, you will need to arrange for the missionary to receive the keys and whatever other information is pertinent. Make sure they know the rules about any cleaning or upkeep to the location before they leave. Having these posted and written down is helpful!

My family was able to benefit from staying in mobile homes owned by several older couples near the United States/Mexico border. They only used them for a few months of the year during the winter, and they offered that we could stay for a couple of nights when they were not occupied. We typically only stayed one or two nights, and our stay was in lieu of paying for a hotel as we travelled. This was not ever a vacation for us, as it was on the path we were taking in our travels, but it was helpful to have a quiet spot to stay and to not have the added expense of a hotel room on our already limited budget.

If you don't have a timeshare or RV, you can still offer to help the missionary rest. Offer to pay for a night or two in a hotel or bed and breakfast somewhere along their travels. You could even buy tickets for them at an attraction close-by. (I would recommend coordinating this with your missionary friends, as they may not have extra days available for other activities or they might rather just choose to actually rest!)

SPONSOR THEM AT A MARRIAGE CONFERENCE

Marriage while doing any type of ministry can be difficult. If you add in the multiple factors that many missionaries face (living far away from a support system, in another culture, and feeling alone) you can have a recipe for a marriage disaster. Stress can wreak havoc on any marriage, but exponentially so for those without a support system.

Missionaries can benefit greatly from attending a marriage lecture, conference, or retreat. You may need to contact them to find out what would fit into their travel schedule before you spend any money.

Ideas can include:

1. A **local lecture or church service** at a church in an area where they will be visiting
2. A **retreat** that is sponsored by a **local church**
3. A retreat like a **"Weekend to Remember®"** sponsored by FamilyLife®. This would be the best option, in my opinion, if it fit into their travel

schedule. There are almost 100 locations around the United States, and you can purchase a gift card online. The missionary can then search the conference locations and weekends and pick one that is best for them. There are some pastor sessions in certain locations, and there are some scholarships available. You may be able to take advantage of a 2-for-1 special that they promote from time to time and buy a gift card for the couple for future use. (They will need to arrange childcare for this and may need to pay for a hotel room as well.)

Time alone as a couple may be difficult for a missionary to find, especially if they are traveling frequently as a family. Offering this possibility may be what they need to revitalize their relationship and strengthen their bonds of marriage.

PAY FOR COUNSELING

Missionaries can benefit greatly from counseling, but not because they are crazy! They experience a great number of stressful and potentially traumatic things. These experiences can vary depending on the country where they are going, the type of ministry they do, their support system abroad, the ages of the parents and children, and their own personalities. Leaving home and relocating in another culture can potentially provoke or exacerbate any underlying tendencies for mental health problems as well.

Parents and children in missionary families will experience leaving family and friends behind, as well as the stress of establishing new relationships at church, school, and in the community. They may not know the language and may find it difficult to understand the culture around them. And this can also happen when they return to their passport country for a furlough or "home assignment"!

Some missionaries may go through a traumatic event such as a robbery, kidnapping, or break-in. Even if they do not have this happen to them, they may live with the constant fear of these things potentially happening to them in the future.

Reasons a missionary (or their children) may benefit from counseling could include:

- Marital conflict
- Parent/child conflict
- Sibling conflict
- Conflict with another missionary
- Conflict with local people they are serving
- Depression
- Anxiety (health, safety, financial)
- Grief (death, relationships ending, missing friends and family)
- Fear (leaving, returning, safety, health, failure, travel, etc.)
- Learning to live in another culture
- Feelings of insecurity and inadequacy
- Returning to their country of origin (whether by choice or because they were forced to)
- Financial management
- Health problems

Giving a missionary the means to visit with a counselor can be a huge blessing. Some insurance policies will not cover this at all, and some only cover counseling expenses after a deductible is met. You do not need to commit to long-term therapy, but even if you offer to pay for one or two sessions the missionary can receive some benefit.

Asking a missionary if this is a need could be a very important, but awkward, thing. It would probably be best if you have an established relationship with the person before broaching this subject, but it could be handled tactfully even if you do not. Church leaders should be able to offer this to any missionary that they support. Help with transitions of home assignment and return from the field of ministry are especially important.

I strongly recommend that all missionaries go through a debriefing or some "re-entry" counseling session(s) when they return to their country of origin. Finding a counselor that is experienced with missionaries returning from the field will be exponentially helpful. Coming back is very difficult when things have changed so drastically, and people are not the same - even if the missionary has only been overseas for a year.

Finding where they belong is often difficult, especially if they are searching for a new ministry or job. Many times, the home church is only helpful short-term and then the missionary is left fledgling – wishing that someone understood their culture shock and would reach out and help them. Sometimes a listening ear can go a long way. Mission committees and pastors should be aware of this issue and offer to fund counseling for the missionary and their children.

You can find more information about the topic of missionaries returning to the United States, leaving the land where they served, and the transitions that they will go through in the book *The Re-entry Team: Caring for Your Returning Missionaries* by Neal Pirolo.

HOW TO BLESS A MISSIONARY

GIVE THEM BOOKS

While there are hundreds and hundreds of books to choose from, in the lists below you will find some ideas to get you started. Don't forget that you can always ask your missionary if they prefer a paperback or eBook. Giving a new book is always special, but passing on a used book works well, too!

Books about Marriage
- *The 5 Love Languages: The Secret to Love that Lasts* by Gary Chapman
- *Intended for Pleasure* by Dr. Ed Wheat
- *Night Light: A Devotional for Couples* by James Dobson
- *The Power of a Praying Wife* by Stormie Omartian
- *Sheet Music: Uncovering the Secrets of Sexual Intimacy in Marriage* by Dr. Kevin Leman

Books about Family/Parenting

- *Give Your Child the World: Raising Globally Minded Kids One Book at a Time* by Jamie C. Martin
- *The 5 Love Languages of Children* by Gary Chapman and Ross Campbell
- *The Jesus Storybook Bible: Every Story Whispers His Name* by Sally Lloyd-Jones
- *The Love Dare for Parents* by Stephen Kendrick
- *Shepherding a Child's Heart* by Tedd Tripp

Books about Theology/Apologetics

- *Basic Christianity* by John Stott
- *The Case for Christ: A Journalist's Personal Investigation of the Evidence for Jesus* by Lee Strobel
- *The Holiness of God* by R. C. Sproul
- *Mere Christianity* by C. S. Lewis
- *Systematic Theology* by Wayne Grudem
- *The Weight of Glory* by C. S. Lewis

Books for Kids

- *Anne of Green Gables* by L.M. Montgomery
- *The Boxcar Children* by Gertrude Chandler Warner
- *Charlotte's Web* by E. B. White
- *The Chronicles of Narnia Series* by C. S. Lewis
- *Curious George* by H.A. Rey
- *The Door in the Dragon's Throat (The Cooper Kids Adventures, #1)* by Frank E. Peretti
- *The Hobbit* by J.R.R. Tolkien

- *The Jesus Storybook Bible: Every Story Whispers His Name* by Sarah Lloyd-Jones
- *Little House on the Prairie* by Laura Ingalls-Wilder
- *Little Women* by Louisa May Alcott
- *My ABC Bible Verses* by Susan Hunt
- *The Pilgrim's Progress* by John Bunyan
- *Treasure Island* by Robert Louis Stevenson
- *The Trumpet of the Swan* by E. B. White
- *The Velveteen Rabbit* by Margery Williams

You will likely have your own favorites. Feel free to add them to the list!

You might also think about adding books that the missionary could find helpful, such as books about gardening, plumbing, electrical repair, aircraft repair, etc. The more you get to know your missionary, the more you will come to know what books or ideas might interest them the most.

If you know they love to read, make sure they know about any local book sales at the library and local book stores when they are in town. They might just find a treasure!

An idea for when you are not sure what books they own, or if sending books to them is difficult, is to buy a gift card to a bookstore or a website where books are available and tell them to pick out their own. Then they will have the joy of picking out new books for themselves or their children.

Another idea is to host a book shower if you know that your missionary or their kids love to read. You can invite people from the local church to attend and have a list of books as suggested donations. You might even want to have a certain theme – like a baby shower for a missionary that is having a new baby. As long as they can travel with books or ship them, they will probably love to have some quality new books for their little one.

HAVE A GARAGE SALE

Have you been feeling like your house is a mess? Are you excited about the recent trend of downsizing and decluttering? Do you need a great way to get rid of extra stuff?

Use all those extra items to hold a **garage sale** to benefit your favorite missionary!

A garage sale is a great way to make a little bit of extra money by getting rid of all those unneeded items that are lying around. You can organize this on your own or join with a friend, several families, or your entire church. Sell your items for specific prices or just ask for donations…you choose what works for you!

Use the proceeds from your garage sale to:

- **Send a one-time donation to your missionary.** You can probably do this online very easily.
- **Donate the money to the missions fund at your church.**
- **Donate money to support a certain project.** For example, you might give your money to pay for the printing of the Bible in a newly-translated language or

you might choose to pay local workers to finish the church building where your missionary lives.

- **Purchase a certain item that your missionary needs or wants.** This might be a washing machine, clothes dryer, water filter, piano, or any number of things they might be wishing for.
- **Give your missionary a special Christmas or birthday donation.** They might wish they had enough money for gifts at Christmas, and your donation may be the only way that they are able to purchase these. Just imagine the joy the parents will feel when their children are able to open some packages!
- **Support someone going on a short-term missions trip.**

Another way you can make some money if you don't want to hold a garage sale is to put some items into a **consignment sale**. There are some relatively new consignment sales for kids' items, and these are a great alternative for people who don't want to sit for several days watching and tending to a garage sale. Search online for a consignment sale in your area.

Most consignment sales have options where you can tag your own items or have them tag them for you, and then you take home a certain percentage of the sale amount. I recently consigned my kids' outgrown clothes in one where I earned 70% of what things sold for. I tagged the items myself and dropped them off. Then, I picked up what was left four days later. (Items typically sell for higher prices at these sales. Something you might only sell for $1.00 at a garage sale might sell for $3.00-4.00 at a consignment sale!)

Either of these options is great for people who don't have any wiggle room in their budget. If you have been wishing that you could do more to support a missionary but every last penny goes to feed your family and keep a roof over your head, this is a great way to be able to do something amazing and help!

Have you ever had a garage sale to benefit a missionary? Think about doing this in your upcoming garage sale season.

HOST A SHOWER FOR THEM

There are many possible reasons that you might consider hosting a shower for a missionary. A shower can be done in person when they are visiting your area, or you might choose to have a virtual shower where a group of people communicate through social media or email to coordinate a way to bless a missionary. You could coordinate a shower through your local congregation, Sunday School class, or small group. Here are some ideas:

- **Home Shower or Kitchen Shower** - If your missionary is returning to their passport country for home-assignment or if they are returning from the ministry abroad to stay stateside, you might want to host a Home Shower or Kitchen Shower. They will likely need just about everything that a family starting in a new home would need. You could choose to have a list of things they would like or have them fill out a registry online for people to choose from. While it might be tempting to give them a bunch of hand-me-down pots and pans that you no longer need, it would be better to keep the shower reserved for new items to make them feel appreciated and special. (Asking them at a later time if they might be able to use some gently used items is acceptable, and most missionaries would be grateful.)

- **Grocery Shower** - If you have a missionary that is arriving in your area for an extended stay, consider giving them a Grocery Shower. It would be a huge blessing to them if you stock their refrigerator and kitchen cabinets. Buy some basic spices and baking goods, as well other nonperishable foods. Include some fresh fruit and vegetables and fixings for lunchmeat sandwiches.

- **Baby Shower** - Hosting a Baby Shower is a great way to show a missionary couple that people are thinking of them and supporting them. Baby showers may not be a normal practice in the country where they live, and they may not have money to buy the extra things that having a new baby might involve. Having them fill out a registry online is a great idea. If you are unable to host a whole shower, having a group of people or congregation chip in for them to buy a great travel stroller might be a good idea. Make sure to find out what sizes of things can be transported when they travel. Consider buying ahead for clothing sizes if they will be away for a 4-year term. The baby will likely go through sizes from newborn-4T during that timeframe.

- **Bridal Shower** or **Wedding Shower** - If a missionary is getting married, you might want to host a Bridal Shower or Wedding Shower for the couple. Again, a registry is a great idea so that you will actually get things the new couple might want or need. Buying them a new vacuum cleaner would not be necessary if they will be living in a village doing translation work on the Bible. Also, keep in mind the travel restrictions on large-sized items. Ideas can include things like small kitchen gadgets/appliances, postage stamps, linens, suitcases, etc.

- **Book Shower** - In another chapter, a Book Shower was discussed. This could be for anyone that loves to read, is homeschooling their children, or for a couple expecting a new baby. All of these are great ways to support a missionary family by blessing them with new or gently-used books to enjoy for many years. You could even do this online, without requiring that the people wishing to participate be present.

- **"Going to College" Shower** - A family that is getting their child settled in college in their parents' passport country will likely appreciate a "Going to College" Shower. You can ask the person for a wish-list of things they might like for school or look online to find lists made for college freshmen. Think about whether they will be living in the dorm or in a house with someone. One idea for a gift could be a gift card to the local college bookstore, but practical things like sheets, a comforter, a lamp, a first aid kit, etc. are options as well. Gift cards for local restaurants would offer a welcome break from cafeteria food.

- **Gift Card Shower** - With any of the above options, you can convert the shower to a Gift Card Shower. You can inform the people invited about local or online stores where the person might like to shop, and everyone can give the missionary gift cards and allow them to do their own shopping. This can also work well if the missionary is far away and will not be in your area in the near future.

GIVE THEM A SPECIAL GIFT

My family was blessed several times by someone giving us a gift during our time travelling to raise support in the United States or when we were actually in Mexico. Sometimes this involved them giving money, but many times it was an item that was very useful to us.

One such instance was a family that gave us a military-grade water filter. They knew that we needed to purchase several large, glass "garrafones" (bottles) of water every week in order to have drinking and cooking water that was safe. They saw a need and decided to purchase this for us. It was extremely helpful and saved us lots of money over the years.

Another example was a Sunday School class that heard that we did not have money to purchase a clothes dryer. By not having a clothes dryer, I grew up helping hang clothes and taking them off the clothes line. It became tricky to get clothes dry during rainy season because you had to wash clothes early and get them hung in the morning. They needed to be dry by midafternoon because it rained almost daily. This Sunday School class took up a collection of money and donated the money to us to purchase a clothes dryer upon returning to Mexico. We had wished for one for years, but hanging clothes out to dry was our only option since we didn't have funds to buy one. This donation was a huge blessing to me and my mom, lessening the workload and time invested doing laundry. This happened during my senior year of high school.

During a visit to a new church, one sweet lady came up to ask us if we had any need for a piano keyboard. We did not know her, but she felt led to ask this as we were sharing our ministry with her church. We had been praying for a way for me to continue to practice my piano playing but did not have a piano or a way to get one. This lady was the answer to my prayers (and we had not shared this prayer request with anyone outside of our family!)

I encourage you to find out some needs from a missionary with whom you have contact. You may be able to give them a gift while they are back in the States raising support, or you may be able to send them a gift of money to purchase the item in the country where they live. Find out the best way to accomplish this. There may be limits on what they can carry or take back, and there may be rules about what can go through customs. Also, they may have to pay extra to get something through customs.

Here are some gift ideas to get you started thinking:
- A new laptop
- A water filtration system
- A washing machine or clothes dryer
- An appointment for family photos
- A kindle

- An iPad
- A camera
- A cordless phone or cell phone
- A car (for them or their child staying for college)
- A gift card
- A massage
- A hair appointment
- A pedicure
- A manicure
- Boxes of diapers or baby wipes
- A car seat
- A stroller
- A breast pump
- A homeschool curriculum
- A musical instrument
- A bicycle
- A tool (saw, drill, etc.)
- A sewing machine
- An instant pot, pressure cooker or slow cooker
- A blender or food processor
- Kid's clothing
- A special perfume or make up

I'm sure that you can think of other items that your missionary might need or want. Brainstorm some other items!

OPEN A MISSIONARY CLOSET

When I was a young girl in the United States before my family became missionaries, our home church was very "missions-minded". We had a month-long missions conference and every service on Sunday mornings, Sunday evenings, and Wednesday nights was filled with missionary updates and missionaries would preach. I can still remember how interesting it was to hear a phone call from "the other side of the world" as a young child.

The church also hosted a monthly evening class called "Future Missionary Fellowship" for those that were interested in possibly pursuing missions someday. They studied different missionaries from the past and discussed trends, techniques, and current mission ideas. My parents attended this class every month.

Because of this focus on missions, my mom helped to start a women's group that was missions-oriented. It was called L.A.M.P. and stood for "Ladies Applying Missions Personally".

They would host lunches and meetings with missionary wives, and seek to bless missionaries when they visited. They were also blessed by hearing the point of view of the missionary wives.

One of the things that L.A.M.P. did was to create a Missionary Closet. They invited people of the church to donate items to the closet, and the church provided a small room equipped with shelves. (It was larger than an actual closet.) Items that could be found there varied with donations, but included such things as new toiletries (toothpaste, deodorant, toothbrushes, etc.), afghans, fabric bags with drawstrings to cover shoes when packing, foods, candies, books, crafts, and small toys. Women in the church handmade some of the blankets and crafts. All of the items were new and there were no hand-me-downs.

Visiting missionary wives were invited to come into the closet and choose one or several items from each section. The "closet" functioned kind of like a store, but no money changed hands. There were no super expensive items in the closet, but many little things that had been donated by church members. This was seen as a way of showing a missionary that they were valued and that their work was appreciated. It was a tangible way for the women of the church to show the missionary wife that she was special.

Consider if this might be something that your church could start. Find out if there is a small room that could be used for this purpose and then start asking for donations. You might be surprised what people will give!

OPERATE A MISSION HOUSE

W e have talked about how much missionaries travel, both to and from their country of service and while home in their passport country. One idea that I have seen both a church and individuals provide for missionaries is a "mission house".

The church that I witnessed doing this provided two homes next to the church building. The houses were church property and the church secretaries were in charge of coordinating the stays of visiting missionaries. The church paid the operating costs of the houses for short visits, and when missionaries stayed long-term they paid the utility bills while they were there.

These houses were used to let missionaries on home assignment or furlough have an inexpensive place to stay and use as a base during their time away from the ministry abroad. They were also used for short missionary visits, like visiting speakers or doctor visits.

In Texas, there was a couple that provided a group of small houses to missionaries that were traveling and crossing the United States/Mexico border. This couple lived in one of the homes, and oversaw the coordination, upkeep, and maintenance of the houses. Missionaries could stay for as little as one night, or they could stay for a more extended time. There was a nominal fee, and the missionary was responsible for leaving the house clean upon continuing their travels.

Blessing a missionary with a house to stay in is possible even if one does not want to do it long-term. If you have a rental property that is vacant and know of a missionary that needs a place to stay, this can be a great short-term blessing. Just make sure to establish guidelines about the responsibilities of the missionary while staying there and the condition that the house must be left in when they leave.

As you can see, operating a mission house can be a way that both a church and a family can bless many different missionaries. You can provide a safe, clean place for them to stay for free or at a reduced cost. Consider if this is something you could provide in the future.

SECTION SIX

* * *

Plans for Blessings

*"Let me hear in the morning of your
steadfast love, for in you I trust.
Make me know the way I should go,
for to you I lift up my soul."*
Psalms 143:8

HOW TO BLESS A MISSIONARY

FAVORITE IDEAS

- ○ _____
- ○ _____
- ○ _____
- ○ _____
- ○ _____
- ○ _____
- ○ _____
- ○ _____
- ○ _____
- ○ _____
- ○ _____
- ○ _____
- ○ _____
- ○ _____
- ○ _____

HOW TO BLESS A MISSIONARY

BLESSING TRACKER

Blessing _____

    Missionary _____

    Date _____

Blessing _____

    Missionary _____

    Date _____

Blessing _____

    Missionary _____

    Date _____

Blessing _____

    Missionary _____

    Date _____

Blessing _____

    Missionary _____

    Date _____

HOW TO BLESS A MISSIONARY

Blessing _____

    Missionary _____

    Date _____

Blessing _____

    Missionary _____

    Date _____

Blessing _____

    Missionary _____

    Date _____

Blessing _____

    Missionary _____

    Date _____

Blessing _____

    Missionary _____

    Date _____

Blessing _____

    Missionary _____

    Date _____

Blessing _____

    Missionary _____

    Date _____

HOW TO BLESS A MISSIONARY

Blessing _____
    Missionary _____
    Date _____

Blessing _____
    Missionary _____
    Date _____

Blessing _____
    Missionary _____
    Date _____

Blessing _____
    Missionary _____
    Date _____

Blessing _____
    Missionary _____
    Date _____

Blessing _____
    Missionary _____
    Date _____

Blessing _____
    Missionary _____
    Date _____

HOW TO BLESS A MISSIONARY

Blessing _____
    Missionary _____
    Date _____

Blessing _____
    Missionary _____
    Date _____

Blessing _____
    Missionary _____
    Date _____

Blessing _____
    Missionary _____
    Date _____

Blessing _____
    Missionary _____
    Date _____

Blessing _____
    Missionary _____
    Date _____

Blessing _____
    Missionary _____
    Date _____

THANK YOU

Thank you so much for reading this book. I am SO excited that you are interested in blessing missionaries! I would love for you to give some feedback about this book by leaving a review about it on your favorite book website! By leaving a review, you are helping others to know if this book is what they are looking for. It also helps the website selling the book to realize that people might be interested in it. In turn, they will promote it more to people who might possibly have an interest in it.

If you are interested in more information about missions, check out my blog at familiesformissions.com for some more great ideas for your family and church. You can find my children's book *Missionary Kid Stories* for sale online. If you would like for me to speak at your church, missions conference, mom's group, or youth meeting, you can contact me through the website.

May God bless you as you bless others!

Jennifer Brannon

HOW TO BLESS A MISSIONARY

www.ingramcontent.com/pod-product-compliance
Lightning Source LLC
Chambersburg PA
CBHW071500070426
42452CB00041B/1950